THE FAST TRACK CCSK

The Ultimate Guide For

Cloud Security Certificate v4

THE FAST TRACK CCSK v4
THE ULTIMATE GUIDE
FOR CLOUD SECURITY CERTIFICATE v4

COPYRIGHT © 2019
ISBN: 9781979768375

ALL RIGHTS RESERVED

visit the author's website
www.ccskcloudsecurity.com

CONTENTS

BEFORE YOU START

What Is CCSK certification and why go for it anyway ?

The Cloud Computing Security Knowledge, or CCSK, is a vendor-neutral certification. It certifies competency in key cloud security areas covering architecture, governance, compliance, operations, encryption, virtualization and much more.

The CSA, Cloud Security Alliance, was the body that released the CCSK for the first time in 2010 and the current version 4 of CSA Security Guidance was released in July 2017 with updated CCSK training and certification exam.

Since 2011, this version 4 represents a major update to the last version 3, including:

- Applied Cloud Security contents
- Real-world Best Practices in cloud security
- Latest cloud technologies, security regulations and approaches
- Integration with other available CSA tools

CCSK is now been adopted as the first security cloud reference and many cloud providers and information security services firms are encouraging employees to get certified.

Cloud Security is a shared responsibility between Cloud providers and Cloud customers. Enterprises are struggling to find security leaders who have the necessary depth of knowledge to set and manage cloud security programs, protecting sensitive information in the new Cloud era.

This CCSK certification book will help you prepare for the challenge with the first cloud security credential, offered by the world's thought leader in cloud security.

Compared to other cloud security certifications on the marketplace, the CSA and the CCSK certification has been listed by Tripwire.com as #1 on the Top 5 Vendor-Neutral Cloud Security Certifications of 2017.
Attaining the CCSK Certification will help you:

- Validate your competence and knowledge in cloud security

domains
- Demonstrate your technical knowledge, skills, and abilities to effectively develop a holistic cloud security program
- Advance to the next level in your career or get a job in the fast-growing cloud security market

Frequently Asked Questions

Gain access to valuable career resources, such as networking and ideas exchange with peers

Q: What is Certificate of Cloud Security Knowledge (CCSK)?

A: CCSK is a web-based examination test of specific competency in key cloud security domains.

Q: What is the latest version of the CCSK examination?

A: The current version of the CCSK test, is version 4 as of this writing.

Q. How long will the CCSK v4 certificate be valid?

A. Your CCSK v4 certificate has no expiration date.

Q. I am already a CCSK Certified on V3 version. Will I need to update to v4 to maintain my CCSK status?

A. No, a certified person of any version of the CCSK will continue to be considered as such. CCSK certificate holders are eligible to receive a special token:

- Free token: if certified between December 1, 2016 and December 1, 2017

- Upgrade token $75: if certified prior to December 1, 2016

Q. Is it possible to take the CCSK v3 of the exam after December 1, 2017?

A. Yes, the CCSK v3 exam will be available for an additional 12 months after the v4 launch, (i.e. until November 31, 2018).

Q: How do I take the CCSK examination?

A: The CCSK test is available online 24 hours a day, 7 days a week. You can register and pay for the exam online. The exam will be available December 1, 2017.The test time is 90 minutes with an 80% score of correct answers to pass the exam.

Q: What areas are tested by CCSK?

A: The CCSK examination consists of 60 multiple choice questions

The exam questions are based on 87% of the questions are based on the CSA Guidance v4, 7% on the CSA's CCM 3.0.1 and 6% of the questions are based on the ENISA report.

Q: What is the cost of the CCSK?

A: The CCSK v3 exam cost is $345 USD. The CCSK v4 exam cost is $395 USD.

Q: How and when will I receive my CCSK certificate?

A: Immediately at the end of the exam, you will get your score and you can download your certificate in PDF format.

New CSA Guidance v4

As of this writing, the CSA has released the version 4 of the security guidance and the certification exam to the latest version.

The version 3 and version 4 of the CCSK exam are still current and available for exam certification and testing.

If for any reasons you still want to get certified on version 3 of the CCSK, you may want to consider my first book on CSA Guidance version 3.

(more information: https://www.ccskcloudsecurity.com/ccsk_v3/)

At the current state, this CCSK v4 book focus more on sharing the content updates that have been released and highlights the latest advances in cloud, security, and supporting technologies. It is a continuation of guidance 3.0 and contains concise and must-read information to update your cloud security knowledge.

For a full detailed guide and contents, you can download the full Security Guidance v4 guide here:
https://cloudsecurityalliance.org/guidance/#_overview

Self-Paced Online CCSK v4 Course

Compared to the previous book for CSA v3, this new book can be used to fully get into the CCSK content and depending on your background and level of expertise in the security field, this might be a good fit to update your cloud security knowledge.

For those looking on a more in-depth and detailed cloud security learning path, the book is a good start but be aware that you need to complete your learning by using the CSA guidance.

Another option that ease this learning curve, is to use my step-by-step guided course to passthrough all what's required to master the cloud security domains.

This online course is an easy-to-digest visual information that focuses on the most important new areas of CSA guidance v4 and presents you the right information for each domain with examples and summaries.

The online course consists of a series of videos with downloadable resources and templates.
By buying this book, you are entitled to receive a 50% discount on the Online Course. (see last for details)

What's inside the Online Course

15+ Videos on CCSK v4 Guidance
5 Exams Simulators
350+ Questions & Answers
2 CCSK Fast Track Books
10+ CCSK v4 Resources
9+ AWS Advanced LABs (Azure coming soon)
24/7 CCSK Expert Support

6 Videos Modules + Course Downloadable Tools & Templates + CCSK Fast Track 4 0 Book + Dedicated CCSK V4 0 Certification Module + Support and Exam Assistance

CHAPTER 1
INTRODUCTION TO CLOUD COMPUTING

The new CSA Guidance V4 documentation introduces a new approach to defining the cloud computing model.

In this V4 version, CSA is trying to harmonize what already exists as standards from NIST and ISO/IEC and what is commonly used by the security field.
Compared to the CSA Guidance V3 documentation, The Cloud Computing definition section will be detailed using three type of models:
- The Definitional Model
- The Logical Model
- The Reference and Architectural Model

The Definitional Model
As a starting point, it is useful to acknowledge the formal definitions from the National and International standards bodies for Cloud Computing:

The U.S. National Institute of Standards and Technology (NIST)[2] defines Cloud computing as:
"A model for enabling ubiquitous, convenient, on-demand network access to a shared pool of configurable computing resources (e.g., networks, servers, storage, applications, and services) that can be rapidly provisioned and released with minimal management effort or service provider interaction."

There is another definition given by the ISO/IEC[3] standards:
"A Paradigm for enabling network access to a scalable and elastic pool of shareable physical or virtual resources with self-service provisioning and administration on-demand."

Also, the Cloud Computing Consumers (or Users) and Service Providers are defined accordingly by:

NIST2 (SP 500-292) with five level terms of the "Cloud Actor":

- Cloud Consumer – A person or organization that maintains a business relationship with, and uses service from, Cloud Service Providers.
- Cloud Provider – A person, organization or entity responsible for making a service available to service consumers.
- Cloud Carrier – The intermediary that provides connectivity and transport of cloud services between Cloud Providers and Cloud Consumers.
- Cloud Broker – An entity that manages the use, performance and delivery of cloud services, and negotiates relationships between Cloud Providers and Cloud Consumers.
- Cloud Auditor – A party that can conduct an independent assessment of cloud services, information system operations, performance and security of the cloud implementation.

ISO/IEC[3] 17788 uses, instead, these terms:
- Cloud Service Customer
- Cloud Service Partner
- Cloud service Provider

Cloud Computing Is Not Virtualization:
Although cloud computing and virtualization may seem similar at some technical level, they are completely different.
Cloud Computing found its roots grounded in:
- Architecture: Ability to provide multi-tenant architectures
- Abstraction: Ability to abstract resources from physical infrastructure
- Orchestration: Ability to automate the provisioning of resources
- Security: Ability to isolate and protect all tenants.

Whereas, Virtualization is more of a monolithic abstraction technology that uses a manual process to deliver required resources.

NIST Cloud Computing Model

The Five Characteristics:

In their publication (SP 800-145)[4], The NIST describes Cloud Computing with five core characteristics:

1. On-demand self-service. A consumer can unilaterally provision computing capabilities, such as server time and network storage, as needed automatically without requiring human interaction with each service provider.
2. Broad network access. Capabilities are available over the network and accessed through standard mechanisms that promote use by heterogeneous thin or thick client platforms (e.g., mobile phones, tablets, laptops, and workstations).
3. Resource pooling. The provider's computing resources are pooled to serve multiple consumers using a multi-tenant model, with different physical and virtual resources dynamically assigned and reassigned according to consumer demand. There is a sense of location independence in that the customer generally has no control or knowledge over the exact location of the provided resources, but may be able to specify location at a higher level of abstraction (e.g., country, state, or datacenter). Examples of resources include storage, processing, memory, and network bandwidth.
4. Rapid elasticity. Capabilities can be elastically provisioned and released, in some cases automatically, to scale rapidly outward and inward commensurate with demand. To the consumer, the capabilities available for provisioning often appear to be unlimited and can be appropriated in any quantity at any time.
5. Measured service. Cloud systems automatically control and optimize resource use by leveraging a metering capability at some level of abstraction appropriate to the type of service (e.g., storage, processing, bandwidth, and active user accounts). Resource usage can be monitored, controlled, and reported, providing transparency for both the provider and consumer of the utilized service.

ISO/IEC 17788, in comparison, lists six identical characteristics, adding the multi-tenancy as another key characteristic.

The five characteristics of the NIST can be seen in the NIST[5] diagram, which shows their visual model of Cloud Computing:

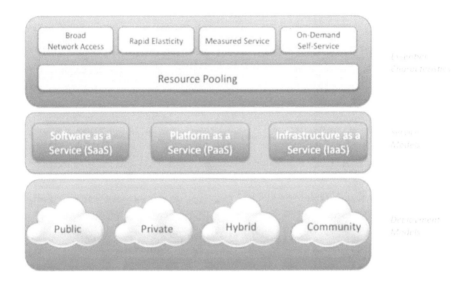

Notice that the "Essential Characteristics" at the top of the diagram include a shared resources pooling supported by the middle layer with the cloud service models and followed by the cloud deployment at the bottom.

We will be detailing each part of this diagram, as it is primordial for a CCSK expert to understand the functions, roles and interactions of each of them.

While reading this eBook, you will notice that Cloud Security Alliance, CSA, is mainly aligned with the NIST Cloud Computing model and used as its core standard.

The ISO/IEC model is also used as a reference, but it will be cited each time to keep it as a reference model.

Cloud Computing Service Models
The three cloud service models are commonly referred to as SPI tiers, which stands for SaaS tier, PaaS tier and IaaS tier.
NIST, in their publication (SP 800-145)[4], also described their service models as:

Software as a Service (SaaS):
The capability provided to the consumer is to use the provider's applications running on a cloud infrastructure. The applications are accessible from various client devices through either a thin client interface, such as a web browser (e.g., web-based email), or a program interface. The consumer does not manage or control the underlying cloud infrastructure, including network, servers, operating systems, storage, or even individual application capabilities, with the possible exception of limited user-specific application configuration settings.

Platform as a Service (PaaS):
The capability provided to the consumer is to deploy onto the cloud infrastructure consumer-created or acquired applications created using programming languages, libraries, services, and tools supported by the provider. The consumer does not manage or control the underlying cloud infrastructure, including network, servers, operating systems, or storage, but has control over the deployed applications and possibly configuration settings for the application-hosting environment.

Infrastructure as a Service (IaaS):
The capability provided to the consumer is to provision processing, storage, networks, and other fundamental computing resources, where the consumer is able to deploy and run arbitrary software, which can include operating systems and applications. The consumer does not manage or control the underlying cloud infrastructure but has control over the operating systems, storage, and deployed applications, and possibly limited control of select networking components (e.g., host firewalls).

Three Cloud service models

NIST Visual Model of Cloud Computing Definition

ISO/IEC uses more granular categories that include seven distinct cloud service categories, including network as a service (NaaS) and data storage as a service (DSaaS).

Cloud Computing Deployment Models

The deployment models are basically the way cloud services will be deployed by cloud providers and consumed by cloud users.

NIST and ISO/IEC are aligned and use identical deployment model.

NIST, in their publication (SP 800-145)[4], described their deployment models as:

Private Cloud

The cloud infrastructure is provisioned for exclusive use by a single organization comprising multiple consumers (e.g., business units). It may be owned, managed, and operated by the organization, a third party, or some combination of them, and it may exist on or off premises.

Community Cloud

The cloud infrastructure is provisioned for exclusive use by a specific community of consumers from organizations that have shared concerns (e.g., mission, security requirements, policy, and compliance considerations). It may be owned, managed, and operated by one or more of the organizations in the community, a third party, or some combination of them, and it may exist on or off premises.

Public Cloud

The cloud infrastructure is provisioned for open use by the general public. It may be owned, managed, and operated by a business, academic, or government organization, or some combination of them. It exists on the premises of the cloud provider.

Hybrid Cloud

The cloud infrastructure is a composition of two or more distinct cloud infrastructures (private, community, or public) that remain unique entities, but are bound together by standardized or proprietary technology that enables data and application portability (e.g., cloud bursting for load balancing between clouds).

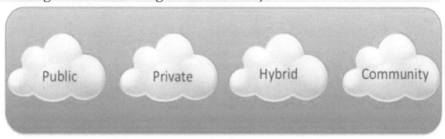

NIST Visual Model of Cloud Computing Definition

Multi-Tenancy

Multi-tenancy is the mode of operation of software where multiple independent instances share the same environment. The instances (tenants) are isolated logically but physically integrated. The Cloud customers can consume Cloud services in a multi-tenant mode with the assurance that their resources are protected and isolated from other tenants.

Multi-tenancy in its simplest form implies the use of same resources or application by multiple consumers that may belong to the same organization or different organization.

Multi-Tenant

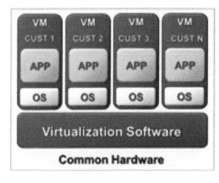 

Multi-tenancy service model in Cloud Computing requires the need for mandatory policy-driven enforcement:

- Segmentation
- Isolation
- Governance
- Service levels
- Chargeback and Billing models for different consumer entities.

Cloud Consumers may choose Public Cloud services that are offered on an individual user basis, or in the case of on-premises hosting with a Private Cloud, an organization may share its common infrastructure between different business units.

The Reference and Architectural Model

CSA Security Guidance has produced a diagram6 that is more detailed and close to real-world deployments. This Cloud Reference and Architectural model describe the relationships and dependencies between the Cloud layers.

Note that this Reference and Architectural model is not a final work, as Cloud technologies are constantly changing and evolving with new approaches, integrations and models.

CSA Reference and Architectural Diagram[6]

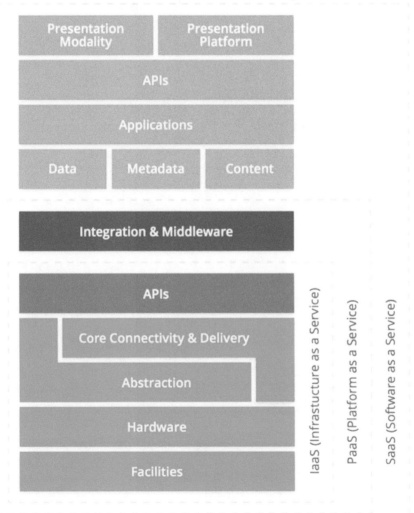

Also, one can have a more in-depth reference architectural model by referring to the documentation in ISO/IEC 17789 and NIST 500-292.

For those who are not familiar with Cloud Computing technologies, I have added a simple diagram that represents the Cloud layers from a high level perspective. At this stage, this diagram is enough to understand the concept behind and how the different cloud models are architected.

The IaaS model is the foundation for all cloud services, with PaaS building upon IaaS, and SaaS, in turn, building upon PaaS.

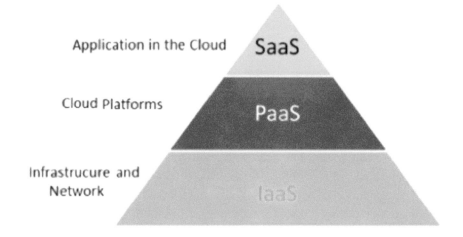

IaaS - Infrastructure as a Service

The IaaS layer includes the entire infrastructure resource stack, from the facilities to the hardware, as well all physical or logical connectivity, including the capability to abstract all these resources (mainly through virtualization).
All these abstracted resources can be orchestrated together and automated to be delivered to Cloud users.

The IaaS also provides a set of management tools (Cloud Management Plane) that manage all components with APIs (Application Programming Interface) using mostly REST (Representational State Transfer) over HTTP as their main communication protocol.

In the diagram below, we can see the different IaaS components: Compute, Storage and Network pools, which are managed through the Management plane using APIs.

CSA Security Guidance IaaS Diagram[6]

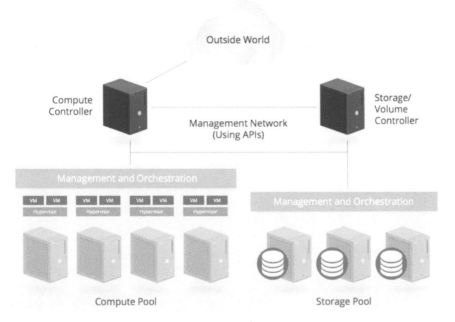

PaaS - Platform as a Service

The PaaS stack sits on top of the IaaS layer and integrates with application development frameworks and middleware capabilities.
These services allow developers to build applications in any language on the platform, without the hassle of the infrastructure management.

In PaaS, the cloud user only sees the platform layer of integration and middleware, but not the underlying infrastructure.

In the diagram below, we can see all the IaaS stacks and the additional layer of PaaS (in yellow) used by all the applications (in green), deployed by developers or 3rd party customer.

CSA Security Guidance IaaS Diagram[6]

Outside World

| Application | Application | Application | Application |

Application Platform

Compute Controller

Management Network
(Using APIs)

Storage/
Volume
Controller

Management and Orchestration

| VM | VM | VM | VM | VM | VM | VM | VM |
| Hypervisor | | Hypervisor | | Hypervisor | | Hypervisor | |

Management and Orchestration

Compute Pool

Storage Pool

SaaS - Software as a Service

The SaaS layer is built upon the underlying IaaS and PaaS layers and provides a self-contained environment that is used to deliver the full user experience, including contents, applications and management capabilities.

SaaS providers build on top of IaaS and PaaS applications that are made ready to use on-demand or deployed on a multi-tenancy model for cloud users.
The Cloud customers, in this case, only use and pay for what they consume without seeing all the underlying stacks. The SaaS vendors (for example, Sales Force) take care of all the applications deployment and requirements: servers, storage, backup, networking, load balancing ...etc.

SaaS vendors can also, depending on their cases, either build everything from bottom-up or use PaaS/IaaS services from other Cloud service providers.

SaaS diagram from CSA[6]

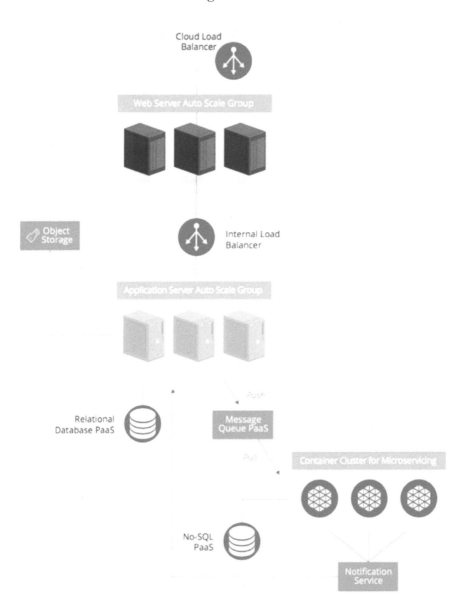

The Logical Model

The CSA Security Guidance has introduced a high-level schematic with a logical model to help identify all Cloud layers based on their functions.

The diagram below highlights the different layers of the logical model definition:

- Infrastructure layer: all the compute, network, and storage components
- Metastructure layer: the management and interface layer between the infrastructure and the rest
- Applistructure layer: all the applications deployed in the cloud.
- Infostructure layer: all the data and information

The logical model is not a new concept, but a new naming to simplify all the layers and their interactions in the cloud.

Logical Model diagram from CSA[6]

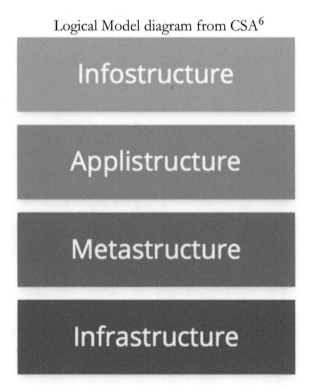

The Jericho and the other Reference Models

On the previous version of the CSA guide, the Jericho Cloud Cube model was used to show the different permutations possible in a cloud offering and to differentiate between the cloud formations.

CSA has adopted a broader approach with a recommendation to different models depending on the area of interest, which is more domain specific (TOGAF, ITIL…etc.)

These models will be used as references and tool to help cover all security domains including:
- The NIST Publication 500-299
- ISO/IEC FDIS 27017
- and ISO/IEC 27002 for cloud services.

Reference Model from CSA[6]

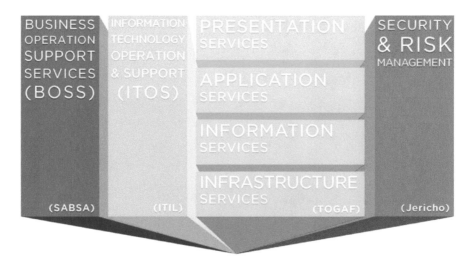

CSA Domains by Categories
CSA domains can be categorized under two main umbrella that covers:

Governance:
These domains are relevant to strategies, standards and policies and are more at the architectural level.

Operations:
These domains are more operational with a technical focus to deploy, execute and manage.

Governance	Governance and Enterprise Risk Management	Domain 2
	Legal Issues: Contracts and Electronic Discovery	Domain 3
	Compliance and Audit Management	Domain 4
	Information Governance	Domain 5
Operations	Management Plane and Business Continuity	Domain 6
	Infrastructure Security	Domain 7
	Virtualization and Containers	Domain 8
	Incident Response, Notification and Remediation	Domain 9
	Application Security	Domain 10
	Data Security and Encryption	Domain 11
	Identity, Entitlement and Access Management	Domain 12
	Security as a Service	Domain 13
	Related Technologies	Domain 14

CSA Domains Mapping

The structure of this book, does not follow literarily the same structure used in the CSA guidance.

This mapping will help understand which chapter cover which domains in the Guidance.

Chapter 1	Introduction to Cloud Computing	Domain 1
Chapter 2 Infrastructure Security	Management Plane and Business Continuity	Domain 6
	Infrastructure Security	Domain 7
	Virtualization and Containers	Domain 8
Chapter 3 Managing Cloud Security & Risk	Governance and Enterprise Risk Management	Domain 2
	Legal Issues: Contracts and Electronic Discovery	Domain 3
	Compliance and Audit Management	Domain 4
	Information Governance	Domain 5
Chapter 4 Data Security	Management Plane and Business Continuity	Domain 6
	Data Security and Encryption	Domain 11
Chapter 5 Applications, Users & Technologies Security	Application Security	Domain 10
	Identity, Entitlement and Access Management	Domain 12
	Related Technologies	Domain 14
Chapter 6 Security Operations	Incident Response, Notification and Remediation	Domain 9
	Security as a Service	Domain 13

* Information in Domain 6 will spread between Chapters 2 & 4
* Chapter 3 contain more information related to CCM, CAIQ and ENISA
* Chapter 6 contain a grasp of all domains

CHAPTER 2
INFRASTRUCTURE SECURITY

The Management Plane

The management plane is the cloud controller of all cloud resources and is mainly composed and managed through:

- API (application programming interface): REST APIs run over HTTP/S
- Web Consoles

Securing the management plane should be the main security concern for any cloud deployment. As the management plane consolidates and centralizes all the management stacks, it is mandatory to secure:

- Who accesses it
- How they access it

Where the management plane is responsible for managing the resources, the cloud user will still be responsible for the configuration:

	Responsibilities	Best Practices
CSP	- Secure the management plane - Provide security features - Granular access to the management plane - Provide SDK & CLI for API integrations - Provide IAM capabilities	- Provide HTTP request signing and OAuth (most secure) - Perimeter security at low/high layers levels - Use MFA for internal authentication - Use granular entitlements for authorization - Provide logging, monitoring and alerting
Customer	- Configure the management plane - Manage all credentials - Manage privileged accounts and access - Use multi-factor authentication (MFA) for privileged accounts	- Mitigate risks of services with embedded password (dedicate API accounts) - Lock down the account owner - Use super-admin account for users - User role-based access (ex: service admin) - Use MFA for users accounts

Infrastructure Security

The infrastructure includes all layers from physical facilities to network, compute, storage, applications up to the configurations and implementation layers. The infrastructure security focuses mainly on cloud-specific infrastructure:

- The Physical layer: ex. Network, compute, storage, etc.
- The Virtual layer: ex. Virtual networks, virtual storage, resource pools, etc.

Network Virtualization Layer

The virtual networks are the abstraction of the physical networks and are used to provision virtual networks in order to segregate different types of networks:

1. Management network: used by the management plane
2. Service network: used by all users (can also be sub-segregated)
3. Storage network: used for backend data traffic

Network virtualization is usually achieved through the use of:

- VLAN: virtual local area networks
- SDN: software-defined networking (find more here: https://en.wikipedia.org/wiki/Software-defined_networking)

NB: SDN offers complete abstraction and isolation boundaries compared to VLAN.

Security Controls

The cloud user is no longer "allowed" to secure the network the traditional, old way. The cloud service provider is fully responsible for the physical network layer, as it is shared between all its tenants. Also, even if possible, cloud customers may not be able to use virtual appliances or virtual agents as a viable solution. These solutions may become a performance bottleneck and cost factor.

The alternative is to use an SDN approach, which will offer:

	Benefits	features
SDN	Isolation Intercept all traffics Meet performance Auto-scaling Elastic licensing Geo-localization Velocity of change	SDNA firewalls Policy-driven TAG tracking Can be tied to the orchestrator Dynamic policies Granular policies Deny by default Encrypt when encapsulating

Micro-segmentation

Micro-segmentation or Hyper-segregation is the approach used to segregate smaller isolated virtual networks to help reduce attacks blast radius and limit the expansion of possible compromise.

The CSA Software Defined Perimeter Working Group has conducted some interesting work by defining a model and specifications that provision virtual networks depending on the user device and user authentication.

Check this link for more information:
(https://cloudsecurityalliance.org/group/software-defined-perimeter/#_overview),

The model includes three components as shown in below diagram[6]:

- SDP Client: used on the device
- SDP Controller: control the authentication and authorization
- SDP Gateway: act as a gateway between the client and the controller and enforce policies

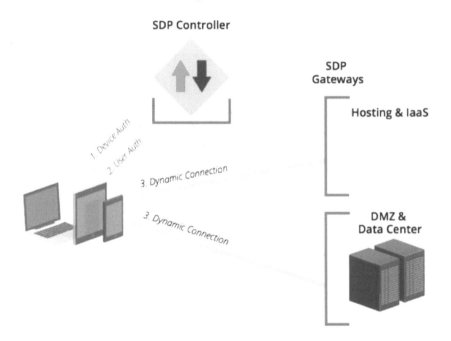

Cloud service providers can use micro-segmentation to ensure:

- Maintenance of the segregation and isolation for its customers' multitenancy
- Continue to provide and expose security controls to their customers
- Ensure perimeter security by minimizing DDOS attacks
- Scrub customer's information at end of service

Hybrid Clouds

Cloud service provider and customer networks are usually not at the same level of security. This difference in trust level, in hybrid clouds, represent a risk factor for both parties. This separation should be enforced by controlling access and protecting segregation using firewalls.

A Bastion or Transit network can be used to segregate both networks and keep a safe hybrid connection:

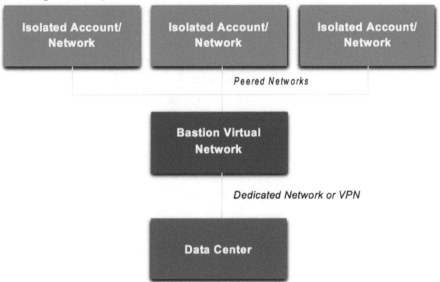

Compute Layer Security

At the compute layer, workloads consume processor and memory resources that run on top of the hardware stack. These workloads can be used by:

- Virtual machines: are instances running on the hypervisors and are vulnerable to all hypervisor's weaknesses (isolation, memory attacks, and secure execution)
- Containers: are restricted environments for code execution. It is possible for multiple containers to run on the same virtual machine.
- Platform-based workloads: are shared platform running workloads for multiple cloud customers. Securing these platforms are usually the responsibility of CSPs.

- Serverless Computing: refers to situations where cloud customers run workloads without thinking about servers or virtual machines. CSP serverless environments take care of all the protections, high availability and back-end.

Immutable Workloads
Virtual machines are usually managed and provisioned through the use of images or "master image". And to simplify, these images are files that reside on the shared storage. The image includes all the things a virtual machine needs: OS, Patches, Config files, common applications…etc. All running workloads on the cloud, in a way or another, runs from this "master image".

Thus, all the patching or security enforcements can be done directly to the master image, which updates all the workloads automatically. An immutable virtual machine is a VM running from a master image, which allows:
- Free patching dependencies
- Expedites the rollout of updated versions
- Security testing integrated into the master image

Immutable VMs require:
- Consistent image creation process
- Integration of security testing into the creation process
- Securing the master image

Immutable VMs can be impacted by:
- Using traditional agents that create performance issues
- Agents that lack auto-scaling and elasticity features
- Agents with additional attack surface and required network ports

Monitoring, Logging and Vulnerability Assessments
The workloads in the cloud are mostly virtual machines and can be very volatile, and may even share the same IP. Monitoring and logging these instance require another IP to track and collect related information. In addition, the logging and monitoring should account:
- The velocity of these instances
- The sizing of these architectures to absorb all information collected and stored

Vulnerability assessments are subject to contractual limitations and usually require that cloud customers notify their service provider prior to any assessments.

The assessment can usually be part of the image creation for immutable workloads.

Virtualization and Containers

Cloud computing has become possible due to the spread and use of virtualization. The ability of virtualization to abstract all layers of the infrastructure and convert physical resources to virtual pool of resources at different layers:

- Compute layer
- Network layer
- Storage layer
- Container layer

With the cloud computing era, security controls have to secure new infrastructure layers, which virtualization introduces:

- The virtualization technology: the hypervisor
- The virtual resources: virtual machine, virtual networks, etc.

Security in cloud computing is a shared responsibility that spans between the cloud service provider and the cloud customer in securing the cloud platform and the provided cloud resources respectively.

Compute Layer

The compute layer is generally composed of resources like virtual machines and containers. Containers are isolated environments where a code can be deployed and executed on top of a shared kernel.

Role	Responsibilities
CSP	Provide and assure multi-tenancy Enforce Resources Isolation Secure underlying infrastructure Maintain an up-to-date state infrastructure Secure the provisioning chain of process
Customer	Implement security controls within the resource Implement security controls to manage resource Monitoring and logging of the resources Image and asset management Ensures the deployment and use of only secure configurations

Network Layer

The network layer in cloud computing uses mostly SDN, but can also make use of VLANs. The network layer brings new challenges to physical network security, the virtual network.

The network layer includes the physical communication between physical resources (ex: Hosts) and the virtual communication between virtual resources (ex: Virtual machines).

Monitoring traffics on these two worlds in cloud computing has to be assured to keep control and secure the cloud platform from any internal or external threats.

This can be achieved by using all the network protection tools (firewalls, virtual appliances, etc.)

Role	Responsibilities
CSP	Ensure segregation and isolation of network traffics Disable packet sniffing Mitigate any metadata leaks Secure the management plane network Provide a perimeter security of the cloud
Customer	Configure deployed resources Configure virtual networks or firewalls Make use of network template for immutable networks Manage configurations and security controls

Storage Layer

The storage layer in cloud computing has also evolved from using traditional SAN (storage area network) and NAS (network attached storage) to more complex and advanced technologies like distributed storage, virtual storage and cloud storage.

Cloud storage provides the ability to keep multiple copies of a data block in different areas or geographical zones.

Securing the storage layer requires the use of encryption to protect data in the physical and virtual layers. But encryption may not protect customer data from the cloud provider.

Container Layer

Containers are different from virtual machine and do not provide isolation. Instead, they provide tasks segregation. They are composed of three components:

- Container or the execution environment
- Controller
- Repository

Securing the container layer is tied to securing the three components:

- Securing the underlying infrastructure
- Securing the controller or the management plane
- Securing the storage repository for the images
- Securing the code executed inside the container

CHAPTER 3
MANAGING CLOUD SECURITY AND RISKS

Governance and Enterprise Risk Management
When it comes to governance and enterprise risk management in the cloud, there are four main areas of interest:

- Governance
- Enterprise Risk management
- Information Risk Management
- Information Security

Hierarchical structure diagram from CSA[6]

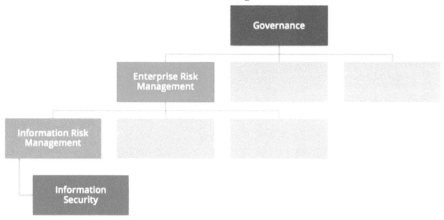

Cloud Governance
Governance is the management practice for all organizational processes, policies and structures, including those related to external service providers such as cloud service providers. The governance responsibilities cannot, in any case, be outsourced to a 3rd party.

Tools used to conduct cloud computing governance are:

- Contracts and legal agreements are generally used to define all responsibilities and mechanisms between cloud providers and customers. In the absence of such contracts, this can be viewed as a governance gap in relation to a cloud service provider. The cloud consumer can still use cloud services if they are willing to accept gaps and associated risks.

- Supplier Assessments: these can be the results of assessments or audits, which include financial information, service offerings, and 3rd party attestations.
- Compliance reporting: these assessments can be internal or external compliance assessments or 3rd party audits and assessments.

Cloud Security Alliance STAR Registry

CSA has established an assurance program for cloud service providers with a set of documentation and assessments like Cloud Controls Matrix and Consensus Assessments Initiative Questionnaire.

Cloud Risk Management

ERM or Enterprise Risk Management is the process that makes the understanding of risk exposure, risk appetite and the capacity to maintain a tolerable level of risk easy.

It includes the process and methods used to quantify risks and opportunities that may decrease or increase the value of an organization.

Enterprise Risk Management for the Cloud relies on contractual agreements and supporting documentation to define the scope of responsibilities and potential risk resulting from using cloud services. The risk tolerance will define the amount of risks that an organization is willing to accept when going cloud.

Organizations have to make sure that Cloud Providers are meeting the level of control required to enable governance and risk management depending on used service models and deployment models.

Service Models:

Service Model	Impacts	Likelihood of Contract Negotiation
SaaS	Risk related to data stored, processed, and transmitted. Significant contract spectrum with smaller SaaS providers	Higher
PaaS	PaaS providers required to share necessary data for SLAs adherence and compliance	Lower
IaaS	IaaS providers can transfer existing governance and risk management activities directly to customers.	Rare

Deployment Models:

Deployment Model	Effects	Likelihood of Contract Negotiation
Public	Reduced ability for governance Reduced ability for Contract negotiation Tradeoff may exist between negotiation and security levels	Very Low
Private	Shared responsibilities and obligations Focus on internal SLA	More control
Hybrid	Issues spanning both environments	Lower

Cloud Risk Assessment Process

1. Request supporting documentation from Cloud Provider
2. Review security documentation.
3. Review all legal, regulatory and jurisdictional requirements
4. Evaluate the contracted service with your information assets.
5. Evaluate the Cloud Provider for the overall services and reputation.

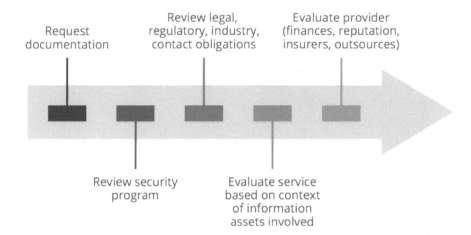

The cloud risk assessment results should highlight all the risks and mitigation actions to be conducted by both parties through a contract or an agreement. For all the residual risks that cannot be mitigated, the customer can either use the Accept, Transfer or Avoid option.

Cloud Legal Issues
In the cloud arena, issues affect both service providers and users.
There are three main issues related to cloud computing that need to be taken into consideration: Functional, Jurisdictional and Contractual.

Data is the main asset for organizations and can be affected in many ways:
- Physical location of Data
- Responsibilities of Data
- Intellectual Property Rights

Segregation of duties between different individuals or groups for:
- Data Controller: Individual or group keeping personal information about their patients, clients or constituents, etc. (ex: pharmacists, politicians and sole traders). They usually need agreement from data subject the rights to collect and use their data. They are also responsible for data confidentiality when a 3rd party is the data processor.
- Data Custodian: Individual or group ensuring the protection and security of personal data wherever the data is located (ex: DBA)
- Data Processor: Individual or group processing the data (ex:

Payroll companies, Accountants)

Cloud legal issues are about the safeguard, the privacy of personal data and the security of information and computer systems. Almost all the countries in the world have adopted data protection regimes that regulate all the aspects of:

- The location of the cloud provider
- The location of the cloud subject
- The location of the data subject
- The location of the hosting systems
- The legal jurisdiction of the contract between parties

By default, national laws will apply to all categories of personal data. Otherwise, all sectorial laws for vertical markets will add their layer of specific categories of data.

Continent	Country	Laws	Compliance Requirements
Asia Pacific	Australia	Privacy Act of 1988 Australian Consumer Law (ACL)	Comply with 13 Australian Privacy Principles (APPs)
	China	2017 Cyber Security Law Cross Border Data Transfers regulations	Security obligations AND Reporting to relevant authorities Data Localization requirements Personal Data has to stay within China
	Japan	Act on the Protection of Personal Information (APPI) Law on the Protection of Personal Information Profession-specific laws (ex: Medical Practitioners' Act)	Consent of the data subject Laws pertaining to specific sectors
	Russia	Data Protection Laws Data Localization Law	Store Personal data of Russian citizens within Russia

Continent	Country	Laws	Compliance Requirements
European Economic Area	all EU Member States All Members of the European Economic Area (EEA)	Directive 95/46/EC for Protection of Personal Data Directive 2002/58/EC for Privacy and Electronic Communications Network Information Security Directive (NIS) General Data Protection Regulation (GDPR) (will apply in 2018) E-Privacy Regulation (will apply in 2018)	-Companies to keep records of their data processing activities -Privacy Impact Assessments -Privacy by design -Privacy by default -Comply with: Data subject's rights -Adequate level of protection -Standard - Contractual Clauses (SCC) -Signing up for the EU-US Privacy Shield -Certification of - Binding Corporate Rules (BCRs) -Complying with an approved industry Code of Conduct -Report any breach of security within 72 hours -Comply with NIS network and information security requirements

Continent	Country	Laws	Compliance Requirements
Americas	Central and South America	Data protection laws inspired by the European directive 95/46/EC	Ensure protection and security of storing and processing personal data everywhere
	North America USA	Several Federal, State or Local Privacy or Information security laws may apply Federal Laws: Gramm-Leach-Bliley Act (GLBA) HIPAA for healthcare Children's Online Privacy Protection Act of 1998 (COPPA) State Laws: Depends on state PCI-DSS	-Requirement of awareness of common law of privacy and security -Adopt reasonable security measures for personal data processing -Apply security measures to any entity that collects or processes personal information of individuals who reside in that state -Have a written contract between Cloud subject and Provider -Notify data subject for breach of security

Data Exchange and Transfers

By default, the data can circulate without restrictions only between countries that comply with each other's defined security level in their national laws.

Contractual agreements that ensure the maintenance of privacy rights for data subjects are required between the data importer and the exporter.

Some countries require prior permission from local Data Protection Commissioner before using cloud services for data hosting.

Cloud Contracts

The relationship between contractors and subcontractors needs to be highlighted, including their liabilities in delivering the service. The contractors and subcontractors must comply with the customer requirement to deliver adequate security controls. Any obligations engaged by the contractors need to be passed down to the subcontractors.

In general, cloud contracts have to include some common principles:

- Cloud service providers are accountable for protecting their customer data under their custody.
- Cloud subject are required to fulfill any agreed contractual agreement with their users, including any privacy notice.
- All Data Collectors or Data Custodians are responsible for data protection even when a third party is hosting or processing the data
- All contracts need to stipulate the permitted and prohibited uses of the data
- All the required measures to be taken in case of stolen or compromised data situation

Due Diligence Responsibilities:

The cloud customers need to enforce these obligations by conducting due diligence or during the performance of their contracts with security audits.

Customer has to conduct internal and external due diligence to assess:

- All privacy policies
- Legal agreements and compliance documentation
- Conduct Periodic monitoring and testing
- Risks from non-negotiable contracts

- Third-party audits and attestations of compliance
- Scope, features and services part of the cloud assessment
- Require the CSP to sign a Business Associate Agreement

Cloud Service Provider	Cloud Customer
-Evaluate respective practices, needs and restrictions, legal barriers and compliance requirements. -Evaluate the cost of doing business in certain markets	- Evaluate respective practices, needs and restrictions, legal barriers and compliance requirements. - Confirm data restricted by law before going Cloud - Confirm confidentiality agreements or data use agreements that might restrict the transfer of data to third parties - Fulfill any signed confidentiality agreement to protect personal information or trade secrets - Fulfill any agreement that prohibits hiring a subcontractor without prior permission of data owner - Fulfill any agreement to which the company is a party, may require the consent of a customer

Cloud eDiscovery

Cloud eDiscovery considerations concern how information will be placed on legal hold, or how information in the cloud will be accessed or reviewed and produced in litigation or regulatory requests.

The "ESI" or electronically stored information definition is as is:
"All information created, manipulated, communicated, stored, and best utilized in digital form, requiring the use of computer hardware and software."

For an eDiscovery process to be conducted in the cloud, this practice can be very tedious for both service providers and customers.
As cloud service providers are becoming more aware of such challenges, they are considering designing a built-in eDiscovery within their cloud offerings.
This built-in feature, known as "Discovery by Design", will attract clients and differentiate their offering from competitors.

For the cloud customers, another option is to invest in on-demand eDiscovery cloud solution either on premise or SaaS solutions.

The litigation holds or best known as "hold orders" is the process where a company is required to safeguard and preserve all data related to a legal action for a discovery process.

This action, if anticipated, can prevent the spoliation or "destruction of evidence, for example", which may have other impacts.

The Federal Rules of Civil Procedure, Rule 26(FRCP) imposes requirements with regard to ESI to the Cloud Service Client and Provider for:

Control	Specifications	Provider	Client	Specific Laws and Regulation
Possession Custody Control	Produce relevant information to eDiscovery Limited to documents and data within its possession, custody or control	√	√	
Searchability eDiscovery Tools	Apply or use e-discovery tools used in Cloud environments. Search or Access all the data hosted in the cloud relevant to eDiscovery request. (limited by access)		√	
Preservation	Undertake reasonable steps to prevent the destruction or modification of data in its possession, custody or control relevant to litigation or a government investigation.	√	√	-Federal Rules of Civil Procedure 37 -Directive 2006/24/EC -Directive 2006/24/EC -Data Retention Law of 2004 Law No. 25.873

Control	Specifications	Provider	Client	Specific Laws and Regulation
Data Retention Record Keeping	-Requirement to preserve and retain data for extended periods. -Document Review or Privilege Review should be possible as part of the eDiscovery process for preserved data.	√	√	
Collection	-Define Client access to its data in the cloud under an agreed SLA. -SLA should specify clauses for extraordinary access in case of litigation. -Litigants can be dismissed from request if determined access to data is not possible. -Court can order discovery if required -A bit-by-bit analysis (or Forensics) can be warranted -Provide evidence that data collection from cloud provider is complete and accurate -All parties can use SLA to determine data discovery when clients are limited in accessing their full data	√	√	FRCP 26(b)(2)(B)
Direct Access	-Cloud Service Providers to provide direct access to the data under their possession, custody or control. -(can be limited due to multi-tenancy or outsourcing)	√		

Control	Specifications	Provider	Client	Specific Laws and Regulation
Native Production	- Use supported data format when Cloud Providers use a proprietary cloud format	√		
Authentication	- Forensic authentication of evidence used in Court to trust that data has not been altered since it was created		√	
Cooperation	- Include cooperation clauses in SLAs for eDiscovery cases. - Provider should offer Cloud services with Discovery by Design included	√	√	
Response Process	- Cloud Provider can receive a subpoena, a warrant, or a court order to access client data - SLA should include clauses for customer notification when subpoena is received - SLA should include timeframe for clients to fight the request for access - Cloud Provider may proceed with the order but need to ensure request is legal and solid prior to disclosing information in its custody	√	√	

Compliance in the Cloud
The definition of compliance in a cloud context is for a deployed cloud environment to adhere to corporate obligations (e.g., corporate social responsibility, ethics, applicable laws, regulations, contracts, strategies and policies).
Compliance is driven by assessing the risks and potential costs of non-compliance with the costs to achieve compliance.

All the resultant mitigation actions needed to correct the compliance state can then be prioritized and initiated.

Compliance Implications

Compliance in the cloud brings requirements for Cloud providers, Customers and Auditors that need to meet:

- Regulatory implications, especially for cross-border data movements
- Responsibilities between Cloud providers and customers, including compliance inheritance and its implications
- Provide enough evidence to support compliance over time

Security controls are used under audits exercises to assess and evaluate the cloud provider compliance. Cloud customers are responsible for providing and maintaining their own compliance status. In the cloud, this can be a shared process where the provider can offset some the compliance requirements from the customer responsibilities. This is known as an Audit Pass-Through.

Pass-Through Audits involves a form of compliance inheritance where cloud providers are certified with standards like (PCI DSS, SOC, CSA CCM) with these limitations:

- Certify only if the provider is compliant, not customers.
- Customer is responsible for its own cloud services compliance
- Customer is responsible for maintaining its compliance

Cloud customers need to review all scopes and limitations of the cloud provider's certifications and attestations.

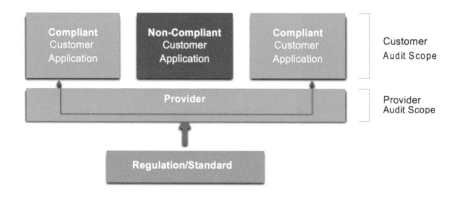

In practice, the cloud security responsibilities are shared; the lower down the stack the Cloud Service Provider stops, the more security capabilities and management Cloud Consumers are responsible for implementing and managing themselves.

Using the previous diagram for the Cloud stack, we can visualize below how the responsibilities shift between the cloud provider and the consumer depending on the use case.

Shared Security Responsibilities diagram from CSA[6]

Infrastructure as a Service	Platform as a Service	Software as a Service

Security Responsibility →

Mostly Consumer   Mostly Provider

The mutual responsibilities between the Cloud service provider and the Cloud customer are contractually stipulated, managed and enforced through Service Level Agreements SLA.
In Cloud Computing markets, we may find two types of SLA for the Customer:

Negotiable SLA
More for private clouds and very in public cloud offers. All the necessary negotiations are done prior to the commencement of the targeted services

Non-Negotiable SLA
In this contract, the Cloud service provider administers only those portions stipulated in the contract. It is the responsibility of the Cloud customer to manage the residual services specified in the SLA, especially when it is either IaaS or PaaS model.
In the absence of an SLA, the Cloud customer can be responsible for all the technical aspects of the cloud services under his control.

Auditing in the Cloud

Auditing in the cloud involves all the tools used to assess cloud provider compliance with internal or external requirements, within the defined scope and statement of applicability.

An audit exercise that generates an audit report needs to specify:

- Audit scope (what is evaluated and to which controls)
- List of identified issues
- List of identified risks
- Remediation and recommendations

The audit report or attestation is legally a statement that mentions audit findings and includes all artifacts (logs, documentations, etc.)

Audit reports can be issued by 3rd party trusted auditors, as cloud providers may not allow customers' internal audit within their premises due to cost and risk factors.

Cloud providers usually share their audit attestation under an NDA (non-disclosure agreement) with their customers.

CSA provides STAR Registry as the central repository for providers to publicly release their attestations.

Cloud customers are responsible for their compliance and have to stay informed about their cloud provider compliance status during the contractual time.

Information Governance

Information can be seen, depending on the case, as Data with value. CSA has a definition for information and data governance, which is:

> "Ensuring that the use of data and information complies with organizational policies, standards and strategy — including regulatory, contractual, and business objectives."

This means that all data has to be handled in alignment with the company requirements and goals. This includes all risks emanating from cloud features and cases:

- Multitenancy: risks from sharing data storage with other cloud tenants
- Responsibilities: risks from sharing responsibilities with different

owners and custodians
- Data Sovereignty: risks from storing data outside the legal boundaries
- Jurisdictional changes: risks from contracts or agreements limiting cloud use
- Data removal: risks from non-compliance with data removal policies

Cloud Information Governance Domains

Cloud usage may require companies to adapt their information governance domains:

Domains	Impacts
Ownership	Data ownership can't be abrogated by a cloud use
Custodianship	Depending on cases, cloud provider may become custodian
Data Classification	To update with cloud scenarios to include locations and handlings
Data Management	To update with policies related to SPI tiers and their requirements
Jurisdiction	To adopt policies in compliance with legal requirements
Contracts	Adapted and required for extending data governance to a cloud provider
Authorizations	To update in alignment with data security lifecycle
Controls	Adapted and required for implementing data governance
Privacy	To align all information management requirements with policies

Data Lifecycle

The data lifecycle is composed of six phases and their key elements are:

1. **Create:** this is the creation phase where contents and new digital content are generated, updated or modified.

2. **Store:** this is the storing phase where the act of committing the digital data to storage repository occurs, and usually happens nearly simultaneously with creation.

Figure 1—Data Lifecycle

3. **Use:** this is the Use phase where data is viewed, processed, or used for processing.

4. **Share:** this is the share phase where information is made available to others, and shared between users, customers and partners.

5. **Archive:** this is the archive phase where the data leaves the active state and enters long-term storage. Usually, it is removed from live data to free and optimize the storage

6. **Destroy:** the last phase is the phase where data is permanently destroyed using physical or digital means (e.g., crypto shredding)

   More information about data lifecycle management can be found on securosis website and their modeling tool:
   https://securosis.com/blog/data-security-lifecycle-2.0

Locations and Access

The location of data in the cloud is an important factor in determining the right security control to apply on the right security boundary. In most cases, data can't be fixed in one environment or location, especially when it's hosted in the Cloud.

The data lifecycle can be viewed as a sub-lifecycle or multi-lifecycle in different locations where data exist, whether internal, external, public, private, hybrid, etc.

Some of the questions that can help understand data location are:
- What are the possible locations for my data?
- What are the lifecycles of my data in each possible location?
- How does data move between locations?

The Access part deals with three aspects:
- Who accesses the data (or Actor)?
  - Client
  - Machine (or application)
- How is the data accessed?
  - Device
  - Channel
- What can we do with the data (or Functions: Access, Process, Store)?
  (See below mapping to lifecycle)

	Create	Store	Use	Share	Archive	Destroy
Access	X	X	X	X	X	X
Process	X		X			
Store		X			X	

The Control part deals with all the allowed or restricted actions for each case and security controls in place to enforce them:

Function		Actor		Location	
Possible	Allowed	Possible	Allowed	Possible	Allowed

Entitlement matrix process

During the entitlement process, the customer should evaluate the different security claims and decide which standards should be applied to the applications and services being hosted with the cloud service provider.

This process should be supported by application assessments with all functional and technical teams.

CHAPTER 4
DATA SECURITY

Business Continuity and Disaster Recovery in Cloud

BC (business continuity) and DR (disaster recovery) in the cloud are related to:
- Continuity of service for any disaster situation for the cloud customer or the cloud provider
- Recovery from disaster recovery that are beyond DR controls
- Process for portability

The resiliency of the cloud against any disaster situation will depend on how all the layers (network, compute, and storage) are architected.
Depending on the cloud provider architectures, cloud customers can benefit from the cloud geo-localizations to load-balance their workloads deployment against any possible outages.

The cloud customer may still need to adapt their applications to be fully "cloud compliant" and benefit from all the cloud features. Depending on the assets to protect, a risk-based approach can be the best strategy to use.

The BC/DR strategy has to define a strategy and process to recover all:

Cloud Layer	Areas
Cloud Metastructure	- Backup all configurations in restorable format
SDI (software-defined infrastructure)	- Create infrastructure templates - Use APIs to orchestrate the configurations
Infrastructure	- Use cloud geo-localization - Redesign application to be cloud compliant
Infostructure	- Manage data synchronization between locations
Applistructure	- Manage all applications codes, queues, etc. - Redesign application to gracefully fail in disaster situation - Use "chaos engineering" to build resiliency

Other Risks

Risks	Mitigation
Lock-in	- Migrate to different providers - Accept the risks - Use graceful failure with APIs responses
Contractual	- Assess contractual requirements - Assess data residency - Confirm RTOs and RPOs

Storage Architectures
Logical vs Physical locations of data

Due to all the potential regulatory, contractual and other jurisdictional issues, it is extremely important to distinguish and differentiate between logical and physical locations for data storage.

Logical and physical data locations are not necessarily in the same location, even if they can. It is recommended that at any given time cloud customers should know where their data is located.

Volume storage

This includes volumes data stores attached to IaaS instances. Usually, this will be represented as a virtual hard drive.

In order to support resiliency and security, volumes often use data dispersion as a common approach.

Object storage

Object storage is one of the latest storage architectures and it is sometimes referred to as file storage.

Rather than volume storage or a virtual hard drive, object storage is more like a file share accessed via APIs or web interface. A well-known object storage solution is Dropbox, which is used for distributed storage.

Database storage

Cloud providers support different types of databases, which can be relational or non-relational—the latter includes NoSQL or file system-based databases (e.g. HDFS).

Cloud platforms provide data redundancy and durable storage mechanisms that often utilize data dispersion and data fragmentation:

Data Dispersion

Data dispersion is a technique that is commonly used to improve data security but without the use of encryption mechanisms.

These sorts of algorithms are capable of providing high availability and assurance for data stored in the cloud by means of data fragmentation.

Data Fragmentation

Data fragmentation in a fragmentation scheme is a file split into x fragments.

All of these fragments are signed and distributed to n remote servers dynamically.

Data migration

Data classification defines all the types of data an organization is handling. This is the first step to allow policies to dictate what type of data should go or not to the cloud and what security controls applies for each type. Tools used to enforce this security and monitor compliance activities use:

Database Activity Monitoring (DAM)

DAM captures and records all Structured Query Language (SQL) activities in real time or near real time. This monitoring tasks include database administrator activities across multiple database platforms but can also generate alerts on policy violations.

File Activity Monitoring (FAM)

FAM monitors and records all the activities for a specific file repository at the user level but can also generate alerts on policy violations.

Cloud Access and Security Brokers (CASB)

CASB or Cloud Security Gateways discovers internal use of cloud service through diverse mechanisms and provides monitoring through APIs and DLP integration.

URL Filtering

URL filtering is used to understand which cloud services, users are currently using from the cloud service providers and accessing them remotely.

Data Loss Prevention (DLP)

DLP is a system that is based on central policies, which identify, monitor, and protect data at rest, in motion, and in use, through deep content analysis using the following options:

- Dedicated appliance or server placed at a network chokepoint between the cloud environment and the rest of the network
- Virtual appliance
- Endpoint agent
- Hypervisor agent
- DLP as a SaaS – provided in a SaaS approach by cloud providers.

Data Transfers in Cloud

Securing the data during a cloud migration or a cloud transfer is a critical aspect that cloud customers should manage very well. Different approaches are usually used depending on the use case for protecting data transfers:

1. Protecting Data Moving To and Within the Cloud
   - Client/Application Encryption: done by an agent-based encryption
   - Link/Network Encryption: done by TLS, SFTP, SSL, VPNs, and SSH
   - Proxy-Based Encryption: proxy encrypts data before sending it to CSP

Data Encryption in Cloud

Encryption uses three components part of an encryption system

- The data itself
- The encryption engine
- The key management

The three components can be in one place or in different areas depending on the use case, design requirements and the threat models.

Data encryption in the cloud can be done at three layers: IaaS, PaaS & SaaS

IaaS Encryption
- Volume Storage Encryption
    - Instance-managed encryption: engine runs within the instance
    - Externally-managed encryption: engine runs in the instance, but the keys are managed externally
- Object and file Storage Encryption
    - Client-side encryption: engine embedded in the application or client
    - Server-side encryption: cloud provider has access to the key and runs the encryption engine.

PaaS Encryption
With Client/Application encryption, Database encryption and Proxy encryptions
- Application layer encryption
- Database encryption

SaaS Encryption
It is a provider-managed encryption using an app and through Proxy encryption
- Provider-managed encryption
- Proxy encryption

Key management in Cloud
Key management is an approach used to secure the data in a cloud deployment and should be closely implemented with adequate encryption protection of all keys used for the encryption.
Four options are possible when it comes to key management:
- Appliance or HSM: using appliance key manager or a traditional hardware security module
- Virtual appliance: using a virtual appliance in the cloud
- Cloud provided service: key management service is offered by CSP
- Hybrid: a combination of the above options

Encryption Best Practices

These factors should be considered with respect to data encryption in the cloud:

- Use data-centric encryption or encryption embedded in the file format for unstructured files
- Use the keys that protect your data and avoid any reliance on cloud providers to protect them
- Protecting data through encryption as it moves to the cloud
- Data should remain protected both at rest and in use once it arrives in the cloud
- Protect files that are often overlooked
- Avoid cases where regional laws may provide undesired but mandated access to your encrypted files

When encrypting data stored in a cloud environment, it is recommended to:

- Use open and validated formats to avoid proprietary encryption formats
- Store all encryption keys within the enterprise. Controlling and managing local encryption keys give assurance that all data has been deleted from the cloud provider at the end of service contract.
- Cryptographic engine for each user or entity should have assigned keys based on identity.
- Encrypt using strong encryption strengths (such as AES-256)
- Follow Key management best practices for location of keys and keys per user
- If an entity needs to share access to data in a group setting, then group-level keys can be associated with the application that maintains group access, and entities within that group can share the keys.

Additional Data Security Controls
Enterprise Rights Management

Full DRM: Traditional full digital rights management using an existing tool.

Provider-based: The cloud platform will enforce controls similar to full DRM using native capabilities

Tokenization, Anonymization and Cloud Database Controls

- Tokenization: This is where public cloud service can be integrated and paired with a private cloud that stores sensitive data. The data sent to the public cloud is altered and would contain a reference to the data residing in the private cloud. Tokenization is less secure than encryption mechanisms.
- Data Anonymization: This is where PII (Personally Identifiable Information) or SPI (Sensitive Personal Information) is stripped before processing.
- Cloud Database Controls. This is where the access controls built into the database are used to provide adequate levels of segregation.
- Test data generation: uses a data scrambling technique to generate similar data as production but classifies non-sensitive data for test purposes.

Data Access Controls

Security access controls for managing data access can be implemented at:

- Management plane level: this is a privileged access management area
- Public level: requires a second layer of control
- Application level: built-in feature to manage access within an application

An entitlement matrix based on cloud platform features is required to document all access, roles and entitlements:

Entitlement	Super-Admin	Service-Admin	Storage-Admin	Dev	Security-Audit	Security-Admin
Volume Describe	X	X		X	X	X
Object Describe	X		X	X	X	X
Volume Modify	X	X		X		X
Read Logs	X				X	X

CHAPTER 5
APPLICATIONS, USERS AND SECURITY TECHNOLOGIES

Application Security

Application security is about how to securely build and deploy applications in the PaaS and IaaS.

The security practice and enforcement in cloud computing, compared to the traditional way, has evolved and benefitted from new approaches, technologies and strategies. The cloud service providers are now able to provide:

- Higher baseline security: to meet all compliance regulations
- More Responsiveness: thanks to APIs and Automation
- Isolated environments: using hyper-segregated environments
- Independent VMs: using micro-services architectures
- More Elasticity: based on immutable infrastructure and images
- DevOps: all practices that create and manage applications and infrastructure
- Unified interface: for management interface and APIs

While all these benefits are real, the cloud customers are facing new challenges:

- Limited detailed visibility: inability to access some logs (system, network…)
- Increased scope: impact of the management plane security on applications
- Reduced transparency: for the operation and integration layers

Secure Software Development Lifecycle (SSDLC)

The SSDLC is the full lifecycle of an application, where all the activities are defined. Industry well-known frameworks help describe in detail the SSDLC:

- Microsoft's Security Development Lifecycle
- NIST 800-64
- ISO/IEC 27034
- OWASP (Open Web Application Security Project)

CSA, from a high level, proposed a macro vision of what SSDLC phases can be in the cloud:
- Secure Design and Development phase
- Secure Deployment phase
- Secure Operations phase

Secure Design and Development Phase
In the design and development phase, five sub-phases exist:

Sub-Phase	Description
Training	- Secure coding practices trainings - Security tests trainings - Cloud service provider platform-specific trainings
Define	- Code standards - Security functional requirements - Entitlements and pre-approved features
Design	- Integration with application architecture - Threat modelling - Secure design
Develop	- Code development - CI/CD pipeline integration - Use of code repositories
Test	- Security unit testing - Security static analysis (SAST) - Security dynamic analysis (DAST) - Security functional tests - Vulnerability assessment

Secure Deployment Phase

Activities	Description
Code Review	-Manual activity that can't be integrated into automation -API calls are scrutinized -Least privilege is enforced -Authentication and encryption are enforced -Notification of changes enabled
Unit testing Regression testing Functional testing	-These are standards developer tests
Security static testing (SAST)	-Checks API calls to the cloud service -Checks for embedded credentials used by APIs
Security dynamic testing (DAST)	-Tests on running applications -Requires permission from CSP prior to testing
Vulnerability Assessment	-Integrated into CI/CD pipelines -Requires permission from CSP or terms of services -Type 1: private Image/Container assessment -Type 2: entire infrastructure assessment -Host-based assessments do not require permission
Penetration Testing	-Requires permission from CSP prior to testing -CSA recommends to use 3rd party firms -CSA recommends to involve developers/admins -Test multitenancy isolation

Secure deployment uses the cloud automation feature to integrate into the deployment process and automate the security testing at the end of the development phase6:

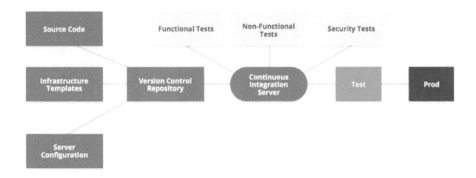

The CI/CD pipelines log and track every code, configuration and infrastructure changes, including testing results. Moreover, securing the pipeline is required.

Infrastructure as a Code

Infrastructure as a code are infrastructures that are fully built using templates and API calls to automate the CI/CD pipelines. The full process integrates security testing and automated provisioning. The production environment under infrastructure as a code is usually provisioned and locked down.

The use of infrastructure as a code improves the security in the cloud significantly.

Secure Operations Phase

Additional guidelines for the operation phase to improve security depend on:

- Locking down the management plane for the production environment
- Setting different credentials for each cloud service
- Monitoring any deviation from the baselines and enforcing remediation
- Using built-in assessment and management features

DevOps

DevOps are the integration between development and operations teams to provide Continuous Integration and/or Continuous Delivery (CI/CD) through automated deployment pipelines.

DevOps provide a better infrastructure management by using:

- Standardization: uses CI/CD pipeline to create Dev/Test/Prod, which is based on the exact same source files
- Automated testing: integrates with CI/ CD pipeline
- Immutable: CI/CD pipelines use and produce master images for the full infrastructure stacks.
- Improved auditing and change management: CI/CD pipelines can track everything and centralize a repository.
- SecDevOps/DevSecOps and Rugged DevOps: describe the integration of security activities into DevOps.

Additional Recommendations

1- Application Design and Architecture

Applications developed and designed for the cloud need to adapt their feature and become more "cloud aware" by:

- Segregation: integrates with the notion of segregation, where applications can run in their own isolated environments.
- Immutable infrastructure: integrates with immutable techniques to secure and recover from any incidents quickly
- Micro-services: use micro-services and auto-scale to assure application scalability and facilitate service lockdown.
- Serverless: support serverless architecture when possible and required
- Event-driven security: integrates with cloud service provider's event-driven code execution feature

2- Cloud Service Providers

CSPs need to make sure that services provided to customers are:

- Hardened against attacks, especially for APIs and web services
- APIs are Monitored
- Protect and Test cross-tenant access

Identity, Entitlement and Access Management

The Identity, Entitlement and Access Management (IDEA), or what is commonly referred to as IAM, need to be clearly defined and documented in the cloud service's design.

Some definitions:

- Entity: can be a user, a device or a piece of code that has an identity
- Identity: this is used by an entity to consistently and comprehensively be identified as unique.
- Identifier: the means by which an identity is asserted.
- Attributes: for each identity, there are attributes that represent the facets of it.
- Persona: is the expression for an identity with attributes that indicate context.
- Role: is similar to persona, or can be a subset of a persona. Identities can have multiple roles, which indicate context
- Authentication: the process of confirming an identity
- Multifactor Authentication (MFA): use of multiple factors in authentication
- Identity Federation: Identity Federation is the relationship between identities and attributes stored across multiple distinct identity management systems.
- Federation: The connection of one Identity repository to another. It is the interconnection of disparate Directories Services. Federation, with the use of SAML, offers portability to disparate and independent security domains with some organizations extending their DS environment via a gateway product that will handle SAML assertions.
- Authoritative source: the "root" source of an identity
- Identity Provider: the source of the identity in federation
- Relying Party: the system that relies on an identity assertion from an identity provider.

Some Standards:

- SAML 2.0: Security Assertion Markup Language is an XML-based open standard for exchanging authentication and authorization data between security domains.
- OpenID 2.0: Is an open standard that allows users to be authenticated in a decentralized manner.
- OAuth: Is an open authorization, an open standard for authorization that allows users to share their private resources with tokens instead of credentials.
- eXtensible Access Control Markup Language (XACML): is a standard for defining attribute-based access controls/authorizations. It is a policy language for defining access controls

Federated Identity Management

Cloud providers and cloud users need to agree on how to manage identities. The CSP has the responsibility to support all the internal identities who access their services along with all the federation services, while the cloud user needs to decide where the authoritative source of identities is designed and which strategy they will use for authentication and control of user access.

Federated Identity Architectures[6]

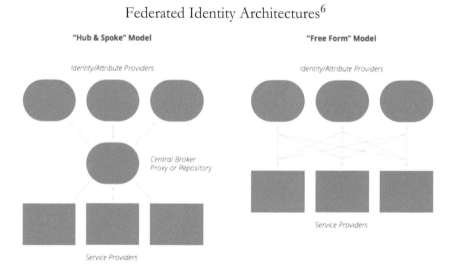

Free-form: internal identity providers/sources connect directly to cloud CSP

Hub and spoke: internal identity providers/sources communicate with a central broker or repository that then serves as the identity provider for federation to cloud providers. Identity brokers handle federating between identity providers and cloud service. They can be located on the network edge or in the cloud to enable web SSO.

It is recommended that authentication and authorization be delegated to the customer's user management system using a federation standard.

But during the design and architectural phase of building the federation identity management system, cloud customers need to consider:

- How to manage identities for all types: codes, system, devices, users, etc.
- Defining the identity provisioning process in the cloud
- Formalizing a process for adding each cloud provider to the IAM infrastructure
- Defining a deprovisioning or entitlement change process for identities in the cloud.

When implementing Identity, Entitlement and Access Management in a Cloud environment, it is also recommended that the cloud customers consider:

- The support for Identity, Entitlement, and Access management that has integration implications for the customer.
- The application's IDEA capabilities to accept a SAML assertion.
- Understanding IDEA requirements of a particular cloud application is a critical part of the requirements definition.
- Identity providers or Service providers may generate tokens such as SAML, OpenID73, or OAuth74 tokens for session caching, allowing a pass-through sign-on capability.
- SAML and WS-Federation: As a general rule or practice, cloud services providers and cloud applications should always accept SSO federation like SAML or OAuth as a standard (or even the less widely accepted WS-Federation).

Authentication and Credentials Management in Cloud

The authentication and credentials management in the cloud is a critical area that needs stronger security enforcement to protect the main door to the assets of a company. Multiple factors authentication is one of the common strategies used to protect against:

- Broad network access where loss of credentials compromises the accounts.
- Collateral damage where loss of credentials in an SSO scenario compromises multiple cloud services.

MFA or multifactor authentication enforces identity authentication using different methods: Hard Tokens, Soft Tokens, Out-of-band Password (phone messages), Biometrics (used on mobility).

One of the World's Largest Ecosystem for Standards-Based Interoperable Authentication is FIDO (https://fidoalliance.org/).

Entitlement and Access Management

Some basic definitions for the entitlement process include:

- Access control: restricting access to a resource
- Authorization: allowing an identity access to do something
- Entitlement: mapping an identity to an authorization and any required attributes.
- Role-Based Access Control (RBAC) model: RBAC is the traditional model for enforcing authorizations and roles
- Attribute-Based Access Control (ABAC) model: allows more granular and context-aware decisions using multiple attributes (preferred for cloud)

A sample Entitlement Matrix below defines the mapping between the roles and the provided services.

Entitlement	Super-Admin	Service-1 Admin	Service-2 Admin	Dev	Security-Audit	Security-Admin
Service 1 List	X	X		X	X	X
Service 2 List	X		X	X	X	X
Service 1 Modify Network	X	X		X		X
Service 2 Modify Security Rule	X	X				X
Read Audit Logs	X				X	X

PDP and PEP in the Cloud

- Policy Decision Point (PDP)

PDP is the authorization layer point that evaluates and issues authorization decisions.

- Policy Enforcement Point (PEP)

PEP is the access management layer point that enforces PDP's decision. The relationship between Policy Decision Point (PDP) and Policy Enforcement Point (PEP) can be shown in the diagram below:

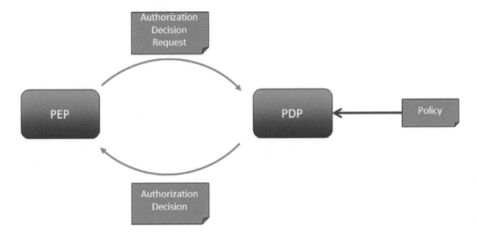

Using the extensible Access Control Markup Language – XACML – PDP and PEP will be part of an overall authorization ecosystem.

Entitlement Process

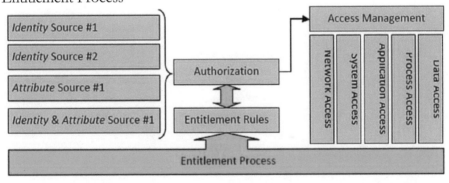

Entitlement and access management processes are a shared responsibility, where cloud providers and customers are required to fulfill different responsibilities

Cloud Providers	Cloud Customers
is responsible for enforcing authorizations and access controls.

responsible for supporting granular attributes and authorizations to enable ABAC for cloud customers | is responsible for defining entitlements and properly configuring them within the cloud platform
is responsible for mapping attributes, including roles and groups, to the cloud provider
ensures that attributes are properly communicated during authentication |

Privileged User Management

Part of the account provisioning and user entitlement are those with privileged access that can access the management plane or administrative areas of the cloud services. These accounts and access controls need to be closely monitored and session-recorded for accountability and visibility.

Third party solutions for privileged access exist with secure vault and enforced authentication to meet higher level of assurance.

Related Technologies
CSA has classified related technologies into 2 wide categories:
- Direct related technologies: those that rely exclusively on cloud computing to work
- Indirect related technologies: those that are seen as cloud solutions but does not rely on cloud capabilities.

Big Data
Big data is a data set of large volume of data, which includes structured and unstructured data. An example of big data might be petabytes (1,024 terabytes) or exabytes (1,024 petabytes) of data.

Gartner defines it as:

"Big Data is high volume, high velocity, and/or high variety information assets that require new forms of processing to enable enhanced decision making, insight discovery and process optimization."

The 3 Vs of Big Data
The 3 Vs of big data are Volume, Variety and Velocity, as pictured below.

Big data is commonly known in cloud computing, as it usually needs and uses cloud capabilities to deploy its services.

Big data can be provided as a cloud service or as an internally hosted on-premise service, but at a very high cost.

THE 3Vs OF BIG DATA

VOLUME
- Amount of data generated
- Online & offline transactions
- In kilobytes or terabytes
- Saved in records, tables, files

VELOCITY
- Speed of generating data
- Generated in real-time
- Online and offline data
- In Streams, batch or bits

VARIETY
- Structured & unstructured
- Online images & videos
- Human generated - texts
- Machine generated - readings

Big data relies on 3 main components:
- Distributed data collections
- Distributed storage
- Distributed processing

Data collection
This includes mechanisms used to collect data from diverse sources. Secure data collection relies on securing all the intermediary storages used to store data during the collection phase.

Storage and Processing
To secure the rest of the components, technologies and principles described earlier are used. Depending on used storage capabilities, security features can be built-in or may need to be layered to secure the distributed data storage from end-to-end and within all data locations.

Encryption and key management solutions can help in the processing phase where data transmission is involved. Encryption capabilities can be tied to the storage technologies.

Internet of Things (IoT)
Gartner defines IoT as:

> "The Internet of Things (IoT) is the network of physical objects that contain embedded technology to communicate and sense or interact with their internal states or the external environment."

This could be anything from fitness trackers, connected lightbulbs to medical devices and beyond. IoT will connect to the cloud for the back-end processing and storage of all the data collected.

Securing IoT can be challenging, as it relies on securing:
- The data collections
- The connected devices from end-to-end
- The APIs used between the devices and the back-end
- The communications channels
- The devices states to stay up-to-date over time (upgrades, patching…)

Mobility
Mobility has to do with all the mobile applications that operate by using the cloud for back-end infrastructure. Similar challenges are common between mobility and IoT when it comes to security:
- Securing the devices (mobiles devices)
- Application APIs

More can be found on the latest research from CSA:
Mobile Working Group
https://cloudsecurityalliance.org/group/mobile/#_overview

Serverless Computing
Serverless computing is a cloud computing service model in which the cloud service provider manages all the server's resources and operations. Serverless security is heavily put on the cloud service provider side, as all the layers of the resources are within his scope. This has to reflect on contracts and SLAs in order to fulfill any compliance requirements.

CHAPTER 6
SECURITY OPERATIONS

Incident Response

The traditional incident response in cloud computing has new gaps to be mitigated and adapted to the IR programs for cloud challenges like:

- How to investigate a cloud attack
- What IR process will change in a cloud scenario
- How to adapt a response plan for a cloud attack
- What the IR lifecycle looks like in the cloud
- Etc.

All these gaps need to be filled while been compliant with the common security standards: NIST 800-61 rev2, ISO/IEC 27035 and the ENISA Strategies for IR.

The IR should be developed from the beginning in the earlier stage of deployment, highlighting all the responsibilities and duties of all parties. This can be achieved by drafting a RACI that will support the contracted IR plan.

The figure below shows the shift in responsibilities depending on the adopted delivery model:

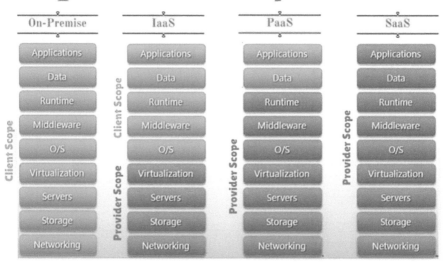

Incident Response Lifecycle

Preparation → Detection & Analysis → Containment, Eradication, Recovery → Post-Mortem

Phases	Activities	Cloud Impacts and Actions
Preparation	Establishing a response plan IR process IR Documentation IR Training IR Infrastructure	-SLAs and its impacts related to the offered standard support -Governance and shared responsibilities between parties -Cloud service models (SPI) and data/logs availability in an incident -IR tools available or "Cloud Jump kit" -Service architecture to sustain an incident (instrumentation, immutable servers, data location, etc.)
Detection	Alerting Scoping and planning Assignments Coordination	-Monitoring of cloud management plane -Integration with existing SOC -Logs availability and gaps -Gaps mitigation with customer tools -Use application-level logging for PaaS/Serverless -Review chain of custody requirements -Automate forensic/investigation process (snapshotting…)

Phases	Activities	Cloud Impacts and Actions
Containment	Containment Eradication Recovery Documenting and chain of custody	-Ensure that the management plane and metastructure are free from attack -Rebuild a clean environment if security compromised -Isolate/Quarantine compromised VMs -Confirm that templates are not compromised
Post-Modern	Learned lessons Improvements and adaptation	-Review what plan did or did not work -Identify limitations in data collection

Incident Response for IaaS

▪ Investigating in an IaaS environment

In IaaS, the infrastructure layer supports and includes all the upper layers, from the virtual machines up to the applications. The cloud customers are responsible for deploying the VM, OS and applications along with their patching and lifecycle maintenance. It is the responsibility of the customer to detect and respond to any security incidents that may arise.

All the supporting hardware servers or network appliances (hypervisors, firewalls, management systems…) are under the cloud provider scope and responsibility for any security incident.

Incident Response for SaaS

▪ Reducing the occurrence of application-level incidents

For the SaaS delivery model, the majority of the responsibility in an IR plan is under the cloud service provider. The customer can optimize the occurrence of incidents by enforcing the requirements for a continuous monitoring through the of logs generation and analysis capabilities part of the provided service.

This will ease the incident response and lower the risks of occurrence.

Incident Management in Cloud

The incident management in the cloud has specific factors, allowing for more efficient and effective containment and recovery in a cloud environment.

This will make the investigation of incidents easier in some respects, as virtual machines can easily be moved into lab environments where runtime analysis can be conducted:

- Data source for detecting and analyzing incidents

The main data source for the detection and subsequent analysis of incidents on the customer side is the logging of information.

Part of the information required is:

- logged information
- consistent and complete information
- cloud's dynamic nature in the logged information
- overall legal requirements
- log retention patterns
- logs tamper-resistant
- logging format
- incident response testing occurrence

Note that CSA recommendation requires that the testing be conducted at least annually.

Security as a Service (SECaaS)

SECaaS is a security service provided by cloud providers through SaaS or PaaS platforms. To be identified as SECaaS, cloud providers need to meet two criteria:

1- provide security capabilities as a cloud service
2- meet the NIST characteristics as described in domain 1

SECaaS provides multiple advantages compared to the common way security is driven:

- SECaaS profits from the redundancy, resiliency and high availability of cloud
- Resource expertise that is readily available and specialized in a CSP
- Intelligence-sharing when the multitenancy provides shared data intelligence to improve the overall platform security
- Deployment flexibility, where elasticity and broad network support evolving environments
- Insulation of clients that protect against attacks and prevent customers' assets from being compromised.
- Scaling and cost-effectiveness with a pay-as-you-grow model.

On the other hand, using SECaaS can present some challenges where:

- Cloud customers lack visibility on how CSP manages their security
- Regulation differences between all jurisdictions
- Handling of regulated data in compliance with jurisdiction laws
- Data leakage in multitenancy or discovery situation
- Changing providers and lock-in issues
- Migration to SECaaS risks and impacts

Cloud Access and Security Brokers (CASB)
CASB are security brokers or security gateways that intermediate all security traffics between cloud customers and their providers. CASB help cloud customers to manage all their cloud provider's services access and security enforcement.

CASB can be offered as a cloud-hosted service with possible DLP functions.
The cloud broker is a third-party that acts as an intermediary between the customer of a cloud service and the sellers of that service.
The broker can be acting as an intermediary between two or more parties during negotiations.
The cloud brokers help with the relationships between providers and their customers by offering consulting and integration services.

Web Security Gateway
Web security gateway is usually used to intercept live traffic before it gets into a company's premises. Cloud customers use this service to proxy web traffic to 3rd party WSG offered as a cloud service to protect against any malicious web traffic.
WSG can be used as on-premise or off-premise solution or both in a hybrid scenario.

Email Security
This is another aspect of cloud customer protection where email services are secured by another layer provided through email security gateways. This gateway provides advanced features hosted on the cloud and integrates with email server solutions.

Security Assessment
Traditional security assessments are fully documented on ISO or NIST standards. But overall, there are three categories of security assessments:
Traditional security/vulnerability assessments in the cloud or on-premises.
Application security assessments: SAST, DAST, and management of RASP.
Cloud platform assessment tools that assess cloud service over API

Web Application Firewalls
WAF or web application firewall is a service that intercepts web traffic for filtering before it reaches the web application. WAF can be provided as on-premise or cloud-based.

Intrusion Detection & Intrusion Prevention (IDS & IPS)
IDS & IPS systems can be provided also as a cloud service or hosted internally within the customer's premises. IDS/IPS monitor behavior patterns to detect anomalies in activity that can present a risk for company assets.

Security Information and Event Management (SIEM)
Security Information and Event Management, aggregates all cloud deployment logs and events data from virtual and real networks, applications, and systems in one repository.
SIEM capability offers a wide range of features ranging from:
- Dashboards
- Compliance
- Data Aggregation
- Logs Correlation
- Alerting
- Retention
- Forensic analysis

SIEM is a major capability that cloud customers need to enforce to keep control of their assets for any cloud deployment.
SIEM requirement for cloud deployments can also be fulfilled by using a SaaS model, but with a different cloud provider (SIEMaaS).
This usually makes for easy cloud deployment with the assurance of a better expertise, automated integration and a shortened delivery time.

Backup and Disaster Recovery

Cloud backup is becoming the ultimate way to perform backup for critical business that needs fast recovery and reliable solution. The days of tape backups, offsite backup services and even disk backups are gone. Nowadays, cloud backup setup is easy and an effective way to protect company assets and guaranty fast recovery in case there is a need to restore the backup.

Backing the data offsite into the cloud in an automated way without the hassle of setting up a full redundant infrastructure to protect the backup sets is a big gain in terms of investments.

The security aspects of storing backup data into the cloud is the main concern for customers and boosts their confidence when switching to the new model if done right.

Cloud backup service providers multiply their offers and services to adapt to customer's requirements and provide enough assurance that their data will be secure. Most of the service providers provide customers with security features covering SSL secure transfers, Encrypted storage, Password protections, Geo-redundant storage, Continuous backup, express restore, deduplication, etc.

One of the best and solid Cloud backup service providers is BACKBLAZE.

BACKBLAZE was one of the first in 2007 to start the cloud backup business, offering unlimited backup storage at ¼ of the cost of Amazon S3, Google or Azure. They were also well-known for their solid API and storage POD shared with the community.

Disaster Recovery services are also well-served by cloud computing. Offers range from many popular DR architectures - from "pilot light" to "hot standby" that enables instant failover.

Cloud service providers with geo-localized datacenters provide a set of DR services that enable rapid recovery for infrastructure and data.

Amazon, with their AWS offer, is currently the most competitive and complete offer on the market compared to other service providers. It provides a secure and certified platform for DR supported by industry audits and standards.

Business Continuity Management

Business Continuity is broader than backup or disaster recovery capabilities. It deals with C.I.A (confidentiality, integrity, and availability).

A business continuity management practice will have a full holistic view of all the three main areas: Technology, Process and People. This model is commonly used to understand the security standpoint of a cloud service provider and its overall approach to security.

This approach will enable auditors' or customers' due diligence to highlight any security gaps that need to be mitigated before proceeding further.

The business continuity management also covers the traditional or physical security of a service provider's facility that was covered in Perimeter security and datacenter operations sections.

Due Diligence

Before transitioning some disaster recovery operations to the cloud, customers should conduct a full detailed due diligence to review the service provider's disaster recovery offer.

Customers need to investigate the internal service provider's capabilities and its team's composition for their crisis communication planning.

The main areas that customers need to cover when conducting a due diligence are:

- Incident response team
- Crisis management team
- Emergency response team (ERT)

Restoration Plan

Part of the due diligence is the review of the restoration plan. The cloud service providers need to provide the documented restoration plan part of a customer's future contract.

The SLA committed by Cloud service providers need to correlate the service acquired by customers and must be contractually documented.

The SLA should highlight at least:

- The RPO (Recovery Point Objective)
- The RTO (Recovery Time Objective)
- The Criticality of the service

FINAL CHAPTER
CONCLUSION

Thank you for taking the time to read this book.

I really hope this book was able to help you understand all new topics introduced by CSA in the v4 Guidance.

The next step is to make sure that you apply the information in this book and review the CSA Guidance recommendations made for each domain.

Free Resource
To help with this last step, I have summarized a short document that aggregate all core recommendations. You can download it here:
https://www.ccskcloudsecurity.com/ccskv4/

Ask me directly
Still have a question or may be need more information on a topic.
No worries, just send me an email and I will be more than happy to assist!
support@ccskcloudsecurity.com

We need you as well
If you enjoyed the information in this book, Please take few seconds and support us on amazon. We'll love to get your feedback.
https://www.amazon.com/review/create-review?asin=1979768374

[CCSK Online Course Discount]
This 50% offer is reserved only for those who bought this book.
You will get an automated coupon based on your Amazon purchase.
(send an email to support@ccskcloudsecurity.com with subject: Book50)

WORKS CITED

1   Source: National Institute of Standard and Technology (NIST),
     http://ws680.nist.gov/publication/get_pdf.cfm?pub_id=9095
     05

2   U.S. National Institute of Standards and Technology (NIST)
     https://www.nist.gov/

3   ISO/IEC
     https://www.iso.org

4   NIST SP 800-145
     https://csrc.nist.gov/publications/detail/sp/800-145/final

5   NIST diagrams
     http://www.csrc.nist.gov/groups/SNS/cloud-
     computing/index.html

6   CSA Guidance & Diagrams
     http://www.csa.org/

CPSIA information can be obtained
at www.ICGtesting.com
Printed in the USA
LVHW070012300719
625829LV00007B/25/P